TE

MUSEUMS

OF DISCOVERY

BY ALLAN C. KIMBALL

The Great Texas Line Press
Fort Worth, Texas

Texas Museums of Discovery

*For bulk sales
and wholesale inquiries
contact*

**Great Texas Line Press
Post Office Box 11105
Fort Worth, TX 76110
greattexas@hotmail.com
www.greattexasline.com
800-73TEXAS**

★ Editor: Amy Culbertson
★ Cover designer: Jared Stone
★ Book designer: Allan C. Kimball
★ Cover photo: Courtesy Bob Bullock Texas State History Museum
★ Back cover: (top) Courtesy of the Johnson Space Center, Houston
(bottom) Cattle Raisers Museum, Fort Worth, photo by Rhonda Hole
★ Title page: Waco Mammoth Site, photo by Allan C. Kimball

Introduction

Monster movies were all the rage when I was growing up—Dracula, Frankenstein, the wolfman, zombies, mummies. They all had the power to frighten us in a darkened movie theater, but even at the age of ten I knew none of them were real. Until I went to a museum.

When newspapers spot a national trend, they try to localize it. Our city's daily paper ran a story about the Egyptian room in a local museum, focusing on the mummy it displayed. I couldn't wait to see it.

There it was, wrapped in millennia-old bandages, lying still in a sarcophagus, its arms crossed on its chest just as they were in the movies I had seen, protected by a glass case—a mummy. A real mummy. Forget all those other pretenders, this monster was real. I could see it for myself. Did it rise at night and stalk the museum hallways? Could it find its way to *my* house?

I went to the library and got books on ancient Egypt and mummies and discovered the most ancient of cultures. I understood the mummification process. I understood the old expeditions that uncovered their burial sites. But still I went to the museum. I went to that room in the museum often. Why? Because it was real. The books were full of information, but they were just words. In that Egyptian room I was surrounded by the real thing, real history. Before me, within arm's reach, was a real mummy.

That's what museums do better than anything else can—they bring us history. We can see it; sometimes we can even touch it. It's not words in a book or illustrations or even photographs. Museums are real. By looking at the real thing, we can make history our own and not have to rely on anyone else's interpretation of it.

I never lost my love for museums. Over the years, whenever I see one, I visit. I've visited the Great Buddha in Kamakura, the Topkapi Palace in Istanbul, and the Vatican in Rome. I've seen the pitiful shrunken head in the Frontier Times Museum in Bandera. I've seen the Spirit of St. Louis appropriately suspended in air in the Smithsonian Institution in Washington, D.C. I've been in awe of the wall of moccasins at the Buffalo Bill Historical Center in Cody, Wyoming. I've seen David Crockett's embroidered vest at the Alamo in San Antonio. I've looked out the same window Lee Harvey Oswald shot from in the Dallas Bookstore Depository building. I've seen the breathtaking golden treasures of King Tut—the ultimate mummy—when they were on tour.

I've seen history. I've seen the real thing, and you can, too. Just go visit a museum.

Texas has hundreds of museums. Whether it's the tiny Toilet Seat Museum in San Antonio or the huge Panhandle Plains Historical Museum in Canyon, every county and most towns have a museum. You can discover history right there. Just listing all of the Lone Star State's museums would require a book five times this size, so I have concentrated on the museums everyone talks about, the ones with unique or important exhibits, the ones everyone should visit. Go discover one.

Allan C. Kimball

Contents

Central Texas

AUSTIN

★ CHILDREN'S MUSEUM

201 Colorado Street, Austin 78701
512-472-2499, www.austinkids.org

Why go? Innovative, hands-on learning.

★ BLANTON MUSEUM OF ART

200 E. Martin Luther King Boulevard, Austin 78701
512-471-7324, www.blantonmuseum.org

Why go? Large, comprehensive art collection at the University of Texas. The Blanton is particularly strong in the areas of Renaissance and Baroque works, prints and drawings, Latin American art and modern and contemporary American art. Novelist James Michener and his wife Mari gave the museum their art collection and its main exhibition space is named for them.

★ BOB BULLOCK TEXAS STATE HISTORY MUSEUM

1800 N. Congress Avenue, Austin 78701
512-936-8746, 866-369-7108
www.thestoryoftexas.com

Why go? The web address says it all: This is the story of Texas, and the Texas State History Museum is the only museum that tells the entire big and bold story under one roof. This museum is less about the preservation of artifacts (although it features several hundred) than about presenting the Lone Star

TEXAS REVOLUTION DIORAMA
Photo: Allan C. Kimball

State's dramatic past in a quick, up-close-and-personal way. The story is told with three floors of interactive exhibits, plus an IMAX theater that takes viewers all across the state, under the ground and into space. Each exhibit shows not just the what-when-where of history, but the why. One presentation that shouldn't be missed is *The Star of Destiny*, in a special-effects theater that will put you right in the center of a hurricane, shake your seat as you witness an oil gusher and vibrate you to the tune of a Saturn V being launched into space. The building itself is properly impressive: red granite with a copper dome and a 35-foot-tall bronze star by the sidewalk. The inside is just as striking, with a four-story rotunda, granite staircase and a 50-foot polished-granite map of the state.

★ LYNDON BAINES JOHNSON LIBRARY AND MUSEUM

2313 Red River Street, Austin 78705
512-721-0200, www.lbjlibrary.org

Why go? Lyndon B. Johnson may have been one of the largest personalities ever to serve as president. This museum celebrates that personality and puts it in a historic perspective. One exhibit traces the history of America during Johnson's lifetime, from 1908

LYNDON B. JOHNSON
Photo: LBJ Library

through 1973—some of the most transformative years in the nation's history, taking America from its pioneering period into the height of the industrial revolution, through two world wars and into a technological explosion that would shrink the world and give us the instantaneous communications that brought the Vietnam conflict right into our living rooms. LBJ's years as America's 36th president, from 1963 to 1969, are also fully explored here; one of the more popular attractions is the replica of the Oval Office from Johnson's years. A relatively new addition is a gallery focusing on

Lady Bird Johnson that includes home movies and recorded love letters exchanged by the president and first lady. One unusual exhibit displays some of the varied gifts LBJ loved to bestow, including stationery, paperweights, coins, letter openers, playing cards and much more.

★ MEXIC-ARTE MUSEUM
419 Congress Avenue, Austin 78701
512-480-9373, www.mexic-artemuseum.org
   Why go? Mexican and Mexican-American fine art.

★ O. HENRY MUSEUM
409 E. Fifth Street, Austin 78701
512-472-1903, www.ci.austin.tx.us/ohenry
   Why go? Home of the legendary short-story writer.

★ REPUBLIC OF TEXAS MUSEUM
510 E. Anderson Lane, Austin 78752
512-339-1997, www.drt-inc.org/museum.htm
   Why go? Artifacts from Texas' time as a republic, at the headquarters of the Daughters of the Republic of Texas.

★ UMLAUF SCULPTURE GARDEN AND MUSEUM
605 Robert E. Lee Road, Austin 78704
512-445-5582, www.unlaufsculpture.org
   Why go? Features sculpture by Charles Umlauf, his students and other prominent artists, in a garden setting.

BANDERA
★ FRONTIER TIMES MUSEUM
510 13th Street, Bandera 78003
830-796-3864, www.frontiertimesmuseum.org

Why go? 40,000-piece collection of Old West, pioneer and prehistoric artifacts. And a real shrunken head.

CANYON LAKE
★ Heritage Museum of the Texas Hill Country
4831 FM 2673, Canyon Lake 78133
830-899-4542, www.theheritagemuseum.com

Why go? So, about 100 million years ago, this burly, toothy acrocanthosaurus was feeling hungry and spied a grazing iguanodon. A chase ensued. And you can see it right here, at one of the best-preserved dinosaur-track sites open to the public in Texas. These dinosaurs left deep footprints in the mud they ran through; over time, those prints were filled in and covered by sediment and became a permanent part of the limestone. But, as today's hilly landscape was formed and the ground eroded, those ancient footprints were revealed. The museum has preserved many of the tracks under a protective roof and added an observation tower so visitors can see them in the proper perspective.

DINOSAUR TRACK. *Photo: Allan C. Kimball*

Inside the museum's visitor center are small displays of Native American and pioneer artifacts. This museum may be small, and fairly obscure, but the 350 dinosaur tracks make it one of the state's most important.

FREDERICKSBURG

★ National Museum of the Pacific War

340 E. Main Street, Fredericksburg 78624
830-997-8600, www.pacificwarmuseum.org

Why go? The recently opened George H.W. Bush Gallery, the centerpiece of a 6-acre campus, is nothing short of breathtaking. Even the exterior snaps a visitor's head around: At the entrance is a full-scale submarine conning tower and bow rising

MAIN ENTRANCE. *Photo: Allan C. Kimball*

from the front lawn. Inside, the museum is exceptional, with many multimedia displays that command attention. The focus is on World War II in the Pacific, from the events that preceded the Japanese attack on Pearl Harbor to Japan's surrender to Fleet Admiral Chester Nimitz, a native of Fredericksburg. One of the very first exhibits proves why this museum is unique: In the Pearl Harbor room is an actual Japanese midget submarine, one of five two-man subs sent into Pearl Harbor with the mission of firing torpedoes at ships during the attack. Light and sound effects flowing throughout the room give visitors the impression of being underwater with the sub. Many displays pair an artifact, such as a tank, with video reminiscences by survivors of a particular battle. You can even look through a periscope to see a ship on the surface of the Pacific. This is one very impressive museum, and one you won't soon forget.

★ Pioneer Museum

325 W. Main Street, Fredericksburg 78624
830-997-2832, 830-990-8441, www.pioneermuseum.net

Why go? To say that Fredericksburg loves its German heritage would be an understatement—and this museum, a collection of 11 historical buildings and hundreds of thousands of artifacts, proves it. The collection provides insight into the settlement of

Fredericksburg and the Texas Hill Country more than 150 years ago. Buildings include the oldest in Fredericksburg— log cabins and stone homes, an old school, a bathhouse, a firefighter museum and a Sunday house (one of the tiny homes the area's German

VEREINS KIRCHE. *Photo: Allan C. Kimball*

farmers built to stay overnight in so they could attend church in town). Also part of the museum is another distinctive building, at the center of Fredericksburg's Marktplatz, the Vereins Kirche. The first public building in town, it served as a town hall, a school, a fort and a church for several denominations. The buildings and grounds are filled with a wide variety of artifacts, among them a stagecoach, a blacksmith shop, tools, works of art, books, toys, photographs and weapons. The grounds also host several special events throughout the year.

KERRVILLE
★ Museum of Western Art

1550 Bandera Highway, Kerrville 78028
830-896-2553, www.museumofwesternart.com

Why go? This is the premier Western-art museum in the nation, dedicated to collecting, preserving and promoting America's Western heritage. Originally called the Cowboy Artists of America Museum, it has expanded its scope while still keeping its focus on art. Displays bring to life cowboys, Native Americans, settlers, mountain men, pioneer women, railroaders and others who created the various aspects of Western history. The collection includes 150 sculptures, 250 paintings and many artifacts. Featured are the works of some of the best Western artists, from Oscar Beringhouse to Fred Harman to Fred Fellows. Traveling exhibits often feature more contemporary work, including photography. The museum is a gorgeous timber-and-limestone building with floors of mesquite wood and Saltillo tiles; the grounds are nicely landscaped and dotted with sculptures. The museum also features an extensive research library and a Western Art Academy providing three-week sessions of advanced instruction.

LULING
★ CENTRAL TEXAS OIL PATCH MUSEUM
421 E. Davis Street, Luling 78648
830-875-1922, www.oilmuseum.org

Why go? Exhibits of oil-industry tools and technology in historical perspective.

NEW BRAUNFELS
★ CONSERVATION PLAZA
1300 Church Hill Drive, New Braunfels 78130
830-629-2943, www.nbconservation.org

Why go? A village of 18 restored and furnished historic buildings preserving the city's German heritage.

★ McKenna Children's Museum

801 W. San Antonio Street, New Braunfels 78130
830-606-9525, www.mckennakids.org
  Why go? Hands-on discovery and adventures.

SAN MARCOS

★ Dick's Classic Garage

120 Stagecoach Trail, San Marcos 78666
512-878-2406, www.dicksclassicgarage.com
  Why go? New museum featuring restored classic cars from 1929 to 1959.

WACO

★ Dr Pepper Museum

300 S. Fifth Street, Waco 76701

VISITORS AT HISTORIC DR PEPPER BOTTLING PLANT. *Photo: Madonna Kimball*

254-757-1025, www.drpeppermuseum.com

Why go? The 1906 bottling plant where Dr Pepper began now documents its history and that of other soft drinks.

★ MAYBORN MUSEUM COMPLEX

1300 S. University Parks Drive, Waco 76798
254-710-1110, www.maybornmuseum.com

Why go? Cultural history and natural science explored in 17 rooms, many with hands-on activities, at Baylor University.

★ MASONIC GRAND LODGE LIBRARY AND MUSEUM OF TEXAS

715 Columbus Avenue, Waco 76701
254-753-7395, www.grandlodgeoftexas.org

Why go? Historic artifacts, from a lock of Sam Houston's hair to a letter carried to the moon to an ancient Bible.

★ TEXAS RANGER HALL OF FAME AND MUSEUM

100 Texas Ranger Trail, Waco 76706
254-750-8631
www.texasranger.org

Why go? Easily the best-known law-enforcement agency in the United States, the Texas Rangers have more than 185 years of their history preserved here. The displays take the visitor on a journey from the Rangers' 1835 beginnings in the Republic of Texas to today, with detours for the Texas

VISITORS INSPECT TEXAS RANGER DISPLAY.
Photo: Madonna Kimball

TEXAS RANGER HALL OF FAME. *Photo: Allan C. Kimball*

Rangers of fantasy—TV series such as *Walker, Texas Ranger*, books such as *Lonesome Dove* and films such as *The Comancheros* and *Extreme Prejudice*. The museum's main focus is on the real thing, however; the exhibits feature everything from badges to machine guns, from Native American items to an extensive collection of pistols, including a few visitors may handle themselves. The Hall of Fame honors the service of more than 30 Rangers, and the museum is the current headquarters for Company F, the largest Ranger company in Texas.

★ TEXAS SPORTS HALL OF FAME

1108 S. University Parks Drive, Waco 76706
254-756-1633, 800-567-9561, www.tshof.org

Why go? A straightforward celebration of the top athletes to come out of Texas, an impressive list that begins with baseball's Tris Speaker, the first inductee in 1951. These greats include Olympic gymnast Mary Lou Retton, football quarterback Troy Aikman, track star Rafer Johnson, shooting legend Ad Toepperwein and dozens of others, all showcased against an interactive history of Lone Star State athletics. Film clips of important moments in that history are featured in the Tom Landry Theater, and memorabilia on display include Hall of Famers' cleats, programs, lineup cards, dolls, jerseys, bowling pins, golf clubs and even a pair of contact lenses once worn by basketball's Slater Martin. Also among the exhibits are Harvey Penick's Little Red Book and replicas of the hands and shoes of National Basketball Association stars—compare them with your own and feel inadequate. The museum also includes the Texas Tennis Hall of Fame and the Texas High School Football Hall of Fame.

★ WACO MAMMOTH SITE
6220 Steinbeck Bend Road, Waco 76708
254-750-7946, www.wacomammoth.com

Why go? Mammoths haven't tramped the earth since the last ice age, about 10,000 years ago, but you can see them today at this recently opened museum—one of only three in North America to preserve their bones. The bones were discovered in 1978 in woodlands along the Bosque River and then patiently excavated

MAMMOTH BONES. *Photo: Allan C. Kimball*

VISITORS SURVEYING MAMMOTH SITE. *Photo: Allan C. Kimball*

over the next 30 years. The museum encompasses two sites, with one now open to visitors. The older site, which has not been opened, has the bones of a nursery herd of 19 mammoths that were drowned in a flood about 68,000 years ago. The open site showcases a male about 48 years old, a female about 20 years old, scattered remains of other mammoths and partial remains of a camel and a saber-tooth cat. What is breathtaking is that the bones remain in place where they were found; the museum built an air-conditioned building around and over the site. Between a small visitor center and the dig site is a walkway through the woods and past stands of sunflowers where visitors are serenaded by cicadas. Museum supporters hope to obtain designation as a national monument so the nursery bones can be preserved and the site expanded.

East Texas

BEAUMONT

★ ART MUSEUM OF SOUTHEAST TEXAS

500 Main Street, Beaumont 77701
409-832-3432, www.amset.org

Why go? Broad selection of contemporary, folk and modern art in all media, including an installation of the folk-art sculptures of Felix "Fox" Harris.

★ BABE DIDRIKSON ZAHARIAS MUSEUM

1750 E. Interstate 10, Beaumont 77704
409-833-4622, www.babedidriksonzaharias.org

Why go? Memorializing the top female multi-athlete in history.

★ FIRE MUSEUM OF TEXAS

400 Walnut Street
Beaumont 77701
409-880-3927
www.firemuseumoftexas.org

Why go? Extensive collection of firefighting equipment dating back to 1856. Hands-on exhibits for children.

TRUCK EXHIBIT. Photo: Fire Museum

★ JOHN JAY FRENCH MUSEUM

3025 French Road, Beaumont 77706
409-898-0348, www.jjfrench.com

Why go? Re-creates the life of a prominent pioneer family in the family's restored 1845 home and grounds.

★ SPINDLETOP-GLADYS CITY BOOMTOWN MUSEUM

5550 University Drive (at US Highway 69), Beaumont 77705
409-835-0823, www.spindletop.org

Why go? Texas' love affair with oil began in 1901 when a gusher came in on a little hill in Beaumont called Spindletop. The rest is history, and that history is right here. This isn't just some generic building filled with artifacts and photographs (although it has those); visitors can view an original derrick and explore several old buildings with interiors restored to the way they were when that big gusher kicked off Beaumont's oil boom. There's an old drugstore, complete with a 1911 soda fountain, a full apothecary's case and a period physician's office. You'll also find two stores, a post office, a saloon, a barbershop and several other businesses. One nice touch is a complete photography studio from the turn of that century, featuring photos of the famous gusher and details of roughnecks working on the drilling rig floor. And here's something you don't see every day: the Beaumont Board of Trade, the local stock exchange. More than 600 companies were founded here because of the oil boom. The museum is also a repository for oil industry research in East Texas, with papers, maps, newspapers and photographs.

OIL DERRICK.
Photo: Spindletop Museum

★ TEXAS ENERGY MUSEUM

600 Main Street, Beaumont 77701
409-833-5100, www.texasenergymuseum.org

Why go? Talking robots present the history of the Texas oil industry and petroleum science. Learn about how oil is formed, how it is found, how it is brought to the surface, how it is refined and its various uses.

BRYAN

★ BRAZOS VALLEY AFRICAN AMERICAN MUSEUM

500 E. Pruitt Street, Bryan 77803

979-775-3961, www.bvaam.org

Why go? Art, artifacts and local histories chronicling the tragedies and triumphs of African Americans in the Brazos Valley and beyond.

★ BRAZOS VALLEY MUSEUM OF NATURAL HISTORY

3232 Briarcrest Drive, Bryan 77802

979-776-2195, www.brazosvalleymuseum.org

Why go? Preserving cultural and natural history and promoting interaction between humans and nature with artifacts, educational programs and a nature trail.

BURTON

★ BURTON COTTON GIN AND MUSEUM

307 N. Main Street, Burton 77835

979-289-3378, www.cottonginmuseum.org

Why go? History of cotton presented in the oldest operating gin in the U.S.

COLLEGE STATION

★ GEORGE BUSH PRESIDENTIAL LIBRARY AND MUSEUM

1000 George Bush Drive W., College Station 77845

979-691-4000, www.bushlibrary.tamu.edu

Why go? A fine museum to help a visitor understand our 41st president, with a couple of unusual touches. Among the artifacts is an Avenger torpedo bomber like the plane Bush flew in World War II (at the age of 19, he was the youngest pilot in the U.S. military); a 1947 Studebaker similar to one he drove to Texas from Connecticut; a piece of the Berlin Wall; replicas of his Camp David and Air Force

VISITORS INSPECT PRESIDENT BUSH'S OVAL OFFICE.
Photo: Allan C. Kimball

One offices; and, of course, a re-creation of his Oval Office at the White House. One touching exhibit shows a simple photograph of a proud father carrying his infant son on his shoulders. The father is George H.W. Bush, fresh from a world war and ready to head out into the unknown of what lay ahead in his life; the boy is his oldest son, George W. Bush. No one—not the photo's subjects, not the photographer nor anyone who knew them—could have predicted when that photo was taken that both would become president of the United States. The exterior of the building is suitably impressive, featuring a monumental sculpture memorializing the fall of the Berlin Wall.

★ MUSEUM OF THE AMERICAN G.I.
1303 Cherokee, College Station 77845
979-777-2820, www.magicstx.org

Why go? Memorializes American service men and women with artifacts — primarily working military vehicles — and uniforms.

GIDDINGS
★ WENDISH HERITAGE SOCIETY AND MUSEUM
Heritage Society: 1011 County Road 212, Giddings 78942
Museum: FM 2239 in Serbin, six miles south of Giddings
979-366-2441, www.texaswendish.org

Why go? Preserves the history of the Texas Wends, Slavic immigrants from Lusatia, in eastern Germany. A group of Wendish immigrants established the town of Serbin, where the historic buildings that make up the museum are found. Tours can be scheduled with a Wendish luncheon.

HUNTSVILLE

★ SAM HOUSTON MEMORIAL MUSEUM

1402 19th Street, Huntsville 77340
936-294-1832, www.shsu.edu/~smm_www

Why go? You know Huntsville thinks highly of Sam Houston when you spot the 67-foot-tall gleaming white statue of him just off Interstate 45, on Texas 75. The first president of the Republic of Texas and the state's first governor, Houston won Texas its independence from Mexico at the Battle of San Jacinto. He made his home in Huntsville, and that home is now a tribute to this Texas hero. The impressive main museum looks like a small capitol building and displays all sorts of items that belonged or were connected to Houston, including his leopard-skin vest and his pearl-handled sword, as well as a diorama of General Santa Anna's surrender to a wounded Houston. Other buildings on the grounds—all containing Houston memorabilia—are his wood-sided log-cabin home with detached kitchen, his log-cabin law office,

SAM HOUSTON'S DEATHBED
Photo: Sam Houston Memorial Museum

his Steamboat House (with the bed he died in), an education center and a newly renovated visitor center.

★ TEXAS PRISON MUSEUM

491 Texas 75 N., Huntsville 77320
936-295-2155, www.txprisonmuseum.org

Why go? When it functioned as the state's primary lock-up,

Huntsville Prison was a place no one wanted to go to: Forbidding red-brick walls; the sound of steel doors clanging shut behind you — even for visitors, it was nerve-wracking. The exhibits inside the prison are designed to educate the public on what real life behind bars is like, despite what they might see in films or on TV. Here is Old Sparky, the electric chair that took the lives of many convicts, but in the same exhibit is information about those opposed to the death penalty. There's art, too: Some inmates spent much of their idle time being creative, and many of the items they made are on display—a ship made from matchsticks, a detailed rose blossom made from toilet paper. Then there are the things you might expect to see in a prison museum—handcuffs, straps, balls and chains. And don't miss the gift shop, where you can get your own Texas Prisoner Bobblehead Doll.

KILGORE

★ EAST TEXAS OIL MUSEUM

U.S. 259 at Ross Street, Kilgore 75662
on the Kilgore College campus
903-983-8295, www.easttexasoilmuseum.com

Why go? History of oil production, including an impressive full-scale boom town.

LUFKIN

★ MUSEUM OF EAST TEXAS

503 N. Second Street, Lufkin 75901
936-639-4434, www.metlufkin.org

Why go? Housed in a historic 1905 Episcopal church, this museum's focus is on art, from an extensive collection of paintings and sculpture by East Texas artists to traveling exhibits. One wing showcases historical artifacts from the area—clothing, furniture, photographs, tools.

★ Texas Forestry Museum

1905 Atkinson Drive, Lufkin 75901
936-632-9535, www.treetexas.com

Why go? Texans refer to East Texas as the Pineywoods for a good reason—the region is covered in 145 million acres of forests, and logging is a major industry. That legacy is preserved in this museum with three exhibit halls, outdoor exhibits and an Urban Wildscape Trail. In one wing you will see logging tools and equipment, an old steam engine once used to power a sawmill and a look at life in an old sawmill town. In another wing are artifacts, photographs and displays about how forests are managed. In a third wing, you can learn how paper is made. In the nicely landscaped area outside are old logging trains, an old sawmill town depot and various tools and machinery used by loggers to harvest and plant trees. The museum is home to the Texas Forestry Hall of Fame and hosts activities for children throughout the year.

PALESTINE/RUSK

★ Texas State Railroad

Park Road 70, Palestine 75801,
and Park Road 76, Rusk 75785
903-683-2561 or 888-987-2461
www.texasstaterr.com

OLD NUMBER 300. *Photo: Texas State Railroad*

Why go? You can't beat a moving museum, chugging through the Pineywoods. The railroad offers visitors scenic excursions through the Pineywoods on steam or diesel trains over 25 miles of track between two Victorian-style depots. The four steam engines were built between 1901 and 1917; the three diesels were built between 1944 and 1953.

NEW LONDON

★ New London Museum and Tea Room

690 Main Street, New London 75682

903-895-4602

Why go? Memorializes the 1937 natural-gas explosion that killed 319 at New London's school. Adjacent to the museum is a functioning old-fashioned soda fountain.

ORANGE

★ Stark Museum of Art

712 Green Avenue, Orange 77630

409-886-2787, www.starkmuseum.org

Why go? A significant collection of American Western and American Indian art and artifacts, including rare books.

SILSBEE

★ Ice House Museum and Cultural Center

818 Ernest Avenue, Silsbee 77656

409-385-2444, www.icehousemuseum.org

Why go? History of how ice was made prior to home refrigerators, along with permanent and traveling exhibits of art.

WASHINGTON

★ Star of the Republic Museum

23200 Park Road 12, Washington 77880

936-878-2461, www.starmuseum.org

Why go? Texas declared its independence from Mexico on these grounds back in 1836, and the Star of the Republic Museum celebrates the history of the republic, which lasted from 1836 to 1846, when Texas became the 28th state in the Union. Appropriately for the Lone Star State, the building is in the shape of a giant star. Inside are a research library; archives; and exhibit after exhibit of artifacts, dioramas and photographs detailing the chronological history of Texas from the first Native Americans through European explorers, settlers and soldiers. One popular exhibit is the Discovery Center, where visitors can experience history hands-on by performing chores such as carrying water, dressing up in period clothing, building a log cabin (albeit a small one) or carding cotton. This is an impressive and detail-oriented look at the people, places and events that shaped Texas.

SLAVE CABIN EXHIBIT. *Photo: Star of the Republic Museum*

Texas Gulf Coast

ALVIN

★ Nolan Ryan Exhibit Center

2925 S. Bypass 35, Alvin 77511
281-388-1134, www.nolanryanfoundation.org

Why go? Showcases the career of Alvin native Nolan Ryan, the best pitcher in the history of baseball and current owner of the Texas Rangers major-league club. Includes a hands-on exhibit where you can catch a Ryan fastball.

CLEAR LAKE

★ Space Center Houston

1601 NASA Parkway, Clear Lake City 77058
281-244-2100, www.spacecenter.org

APOLLO 17 EXHIBIT. *Photo: Space Center Houston*

Why go? The big advantage the National Aeronautic and Space Administration had in starting its own museum is that NASA already had interesting stuff just scattered around. The actual Apollo 17 space capsule, for example, or a giant Saturn 5 space rocket. The museum is part of NASA's Johnson Space Center, the control center for all manned U.S. space missions. One gallery, which traces the history of the U.S. space program, boasts the world's largest collection of moon rocks. Another gallery is kid-friendly, enabling children to build their own space ship or to discover how much they would weigh on other planets. The five-story-high screen in the Space Center Theater brings visitors into the life of an astronaut and takes them on a tour through space. Outside the theater is the world's best collection of space suits, with a gallery of photos of every U.S. astronaut who has flown in space. And if you want to test your own skills as a space pilot, check out the Flight Simulator and land a space shuttle, or dock your spacecraft to the space station. Or check out the "Living in Space" exhibit, where you can get zipped up in a space sleeping bag and learn how showering in zero gravity can be a real problem. One unusual option here is the Level 9 Tour, which takes visitors behind the scenes to see Mission Control and areas where astronauts train. It's a long tour, but it includes lunch in the astronauts' cafeteria.

CLUTE

★ BRAZOSPORT CENTER FOR THE ARTS & SCIENCES

400 College Boulevard, Clute 77531
979-265-7661, www.bcfas.org

Why go? Art collection, performance spaces for concerts and theater, natural-science museum and planetarium.

CORPUS CHRISTI

★ USS LEXINGTON MUSEUM ON THE BAY

2914 N. Shoreline Boulevard, Corpus Christi 78403
361-888-4873 or 800-523-9539, www.usslexington.com

Why go? This floating museum across the ship channel from downtown Corpus will take your breath away, because it once was essentially a floating city. The Lex was a state-of-the-art U.S. Navy aircraft carrier during World War II and served as a training carrier in later years; the size of the ship alone is impressive. Tours take visitors along the flight deck, by the giant chain that raises and lowers the ship's anchor, into officers' quarters and hangar bays, through the Combat Information Center and inside the sick bay and the ship's galley. One entertaining exhibit is the flight simulator where you get to experience what it's like to be launched from a carrier deck and to fly into battle to destroy tanks while dodging missiles. Featured onboard is a three-story-tall-screen theater that puts you into the pilot seat of an F-15 Eagle fighter jet. Youth groups may also spend the night on board the Lexington.

★ TEXAS SURF MUSEUM

309 N. Water Street, Corpus Christi 78401
361-888-7873, www.texassurfmuseum.com

Why go? Surf movies, surfing memorabilia, board collection, surf shop and historic photos.

GALVESTON

★ GALVESTON ARTS CENTER

2127 Strand, Galveston 77550
Call or check website; an ongoing renovation has displaced the museum into temporary quarters at 2501 Market Street.
409-763-2403, www.contemporaryartgalveston.org

Why go? Contemporary art and fine crafts from all over Texas, in a historic building with exhibit and retail galleries.

★ GALVESTON RAILROAD MUSEUM

2602 Santa Fe Place, Galveston 77550

409-765-5700, www.galvestonrrmuseum.com

Why go? Historic locomotives and cars, model train layouts and rail travel memorabilia, in Galveston's original Santa Fe Union Station.

★ MOODY GARDENS

One Hope Boulevard, Galveston 77554

800-582-4673, www.moodygardens.com

Why go? Exceptional educational complex housed in three glass pyramids. The museum portion showcases interactive science exhibits from around the country, but Moody Gardens is far more than a museum. It's more of a nonprofit theme park, with a six-story IMAX screen, a simulation theater and a special-effects theater; paddlewheel boat cruises; a landscaped beach water park; penguin and seal encounters; a hotel, spa and conference center; a golf course; and a mile-long Festival of Lights at the holidays.

★ OCEAN STAR OFFSHORE DRILLING RIG AND MUSEUM

Pier 19, Galveston 77550

409-766-782

www.oceanstaroec.com

Why go? You can't think of Texas without thinking of oil, so this museum would be important even if the disastrous

DRILLING RIG. *Photo: Ocean Star Museum*

events in the Gulf of Mexico in April 2010 hadn't happened. That's when BP Oil's Deepwater Horizon offshore rig exploded, causing the largest marine oil spill in history. With a visit to the Ocean Star, you can learn what life is like on an offshore rig and how oil is brought up through the ocean depths. Built in 1969, the now-retired rig once worked the Gulf of Mexico. Equipment, displays and photographs teach about geological exploration, drilling and oil and gas production. One fascinating exhibit gives you a fish-eye view of how a drilling rig and its pipes function. Outside is a variety of equipment, including a blowout preventer, drill pipe, cementing unit and robotic underwater manipulator. Up top are the classic drilling rig and drilling floor to be explored. The Hall of Fame inside honors people instrumental in taking oil drilling offshore and showcases pioneering technology.

★ Texas Seaport Museum

Pier 21, No. 8, Galveston 77550
409-763-1877, www.galvestonhistory.org/Texas_Seaport_Museum.asp

Why go? The big draw here is the 1877 barque Elissa, with her three masts, 19 sails and gleaming wood lovingly restored. Adjacent

SAILING SHIP ELISSA AT SEAPORT MUSEUM. *Photo: Allan C. Kimball*

to this floating beauty is a museum and theater devoted to the history of seaborne commerce and immigration in the area. If immigrants came to Texas by sea, Galveston was usually where they debarked. And admission to the museum includes access to the Galveston

Immigrant Database containing the names of 133,000 immigrants. Visitors can use it to look for ancestors' names.

HOUSTON

★ BUFFALO SOLDIERS NATIONAL MUSEUM

1834 Southmore Boulevard, Houston 77004
713-942-8920
www.buffalosoldiermuseum.com

Why go? Blacks have fought for America in every conflict from the Revolutionary War to today's Middle East campaigns. They've even flown into space. And this is one of the few museums in the United States dedicated solely to preserving the history of African-American soldiers. (The term "Buffalo Soldiers" was coined by Native Americans to describe black soldiers during the Indian Wars of the late 19th

BLACK ASTRONAUTS EXHIBIT.
Photo: Buffalo Soldier Museum

century.) That the museum is situated in Houston is appropriate, considering the 1917 riot involving soldiers from the 24th Negro Infantry Regiment stationed at Camp Logan. Artifacts from the camp are on display at the museum, along with memorabilia from every era of military service.

★ CHILDREN'S MUSEUM OF HOUSTON

1500 Binz Street, Houston 77004
713-522-1138, www.cmhouston.org

Why go? A multitude of hands-on, interactive educational exhibits in a whimsical building in Houston's museum district.

★ HEALTH MUSEUM

1515 Hermann Drive, Houston 77004
713-521-1515, www.thehealthmuseum.org

Why go? Where else can you take a stroll through the human body? And have a hands-on experience while you do? The museum's Amazing Body Pavilion has 61 interactive video and audio exhibits; a 22-foot-long backbone, complete with ribs, to give visitors the feeling of being inside a giant ribcage; the 27-foot intestine; and a walk-through brain complete with memory games. Look down a throat and watch vocal cords in action; visit clogged arteries; walk into an eyeball; watch a skeleton riding a bicycle—all in just one pavilion. You'll also find exhibits on health and medical sciences, films in 3-D and 4-D (that's 3-D with added special effects like lightning), animal organ dissections, live science shows, science labs and workshops. "You: The Exhibit" is the latest feature,

THE BONE ROOM. *Photo: Houston Health Museum*

showing you what your internal organs look like, how you might look if you were a different gender or race, how you will look in 30 years and how you might look if you smoked or ate too much. You cannot be bored for even a second at this museum.

★ HOLOCAUST MUSEUM HOUSTON

5401 Caroline Street, Houston 77004
713-942-8000, www.hmh.org

Why go? Memorializes the 6 million Jews and other innocent people killed by the Nazis during World War II, with film, photographs, documents and impressive artifacts, including a rare Danish rescue boat.

★ HOUSTON MUSEUM OF NATURAL SCIENCE

5555 Hermann Park Drive, Houston 77030
713-639-4629, www.hmns.org

Why go? Now more than 100 years old, the museum focuses on science of all sorts, from astronomy and anthropology to entomology and energy to zoology. Children love the Cockrell Butterfly Center, a rain-forest replica filled with hundreds of butterflies from around the world in a three-story glass enclosure built around a 50-foot waterfall. The Hall of the Americas features impressively large displays on indigenous New World peoples, while another hall focuses on the ancients of the Old World, complete with Egyptian mummy. Another hall takes you into the inner world of chemical reactions to show you how your own body works; yet another takes you into space with exhibits of moon rocks and spacecraft. At the Burke-Baker Planetarium, visitors can settle back and watch the sky unfold above and around them, visiting stars and planets and asteroids. And if a simulated star show isn't enough, head over to the George Observatory, an hour south of Houston at Brazos Bend State Park, where you can see the real thing through state-of-the-art telescopes. There's a much smaller satellite museum facility southwest of Houston at Sugar Land.

★ THE MENIL COLLECTION

1515 Sul Ross Street, Houston 77006
713-525-9400, www.menil.org

Why go? The range of this legendary collection is exhaustive, showing a clear connection between ancient and contemporary art. The Menil Collection was founded by John and Dominique de Menil, who fled France during World War II, eventually making their way to Houston, world headquarters of the Schlumberger oil-services company founded by Dominique's father. Passionate about the spiritual role of art, they began collecting in earnest, eventually focusing on European and contemporary American works. The centerpiece of the museum campus is Renzo Piano's "leaf"-roofed building, his first American commission, designed to blend in with the surrounding residential neighborhood. Several other satellite buildings are clustered in this inner-city neighborhood of parks and bungalows. Many of the bungalows are now Menil offices or homes to other arts groups; nearly all are painted the signature Menil gray. The main building displays rotating exhibits from the museum's collection of 16,000 works of art, from the antiquities and tribal art through contemporary. One of the satellite buildings is the Rothko Chapel, a nondenominational place of meditation that houses several paintings by Mark Rothko—subtle variations in color on large canvases. In a reflecting pool outside the chapel is Barnett Newman's famed "Broken Obelisk" sculpture, dedicated to the memory of Martin Luther King Jr. Other buildings and gardens host the works of contemporary artists Cy Twombly, Dan Flavin, Michael Helzer, Jim Love and more; a new chapel houses ancient Byzantine frescoes from Cyprus in a stark modern building.

RITIME MUSEUM and port. *Photo: Allan C. Kimball*

have a panoramic view of the port of Rockport, adjacent
ansas and a portion of the Intercoastal Waterway. The
shows classic seafaring films every Friday.

TEXAS CITY

CITY MUSEUM
Street N., Texas City 77590
660, 409-643-5799, www.texas-city-tx.org/Museum/
out.htm
Focuses on the history of the city, the birth of the
rce, and the 1947 explosion that killed 581 people
ted the town. Hands-on children's exhibits include a
The museum is also home to the Galveston County
ad Club with an impressive layout on display.

★ MUSEUM OF FINE ARTS, HOUSTON
1001 Bissonnet, Houston 77005
713-639-7300, www.mfah.org

Why go? One of the largest art museums in America, the MFAH has a main campus comprising two main museum buildings, two art schools and a sculpture garden in the city's museum district. Its art library is the largest in the Southwest. Also under the MFAH umbrella in Houston are the impressive Bayou Bend Collection of decorative and fine arts, including 14 acres of gardens, and the Rienzi house, with its European decorative-art collection and more than four acres of gardens. The MFAH has a worldwide reputation, and its collection of 63,000 works of art explains why—from centuries-old masterpieces to modern art. Its extensive fabric collection features quilts, needlework and clothing from designers such as Oscar de la Renta and Yves Saint Laurent. Its photography works flow from the very beginnings of the technology through European photo art in the early 20th century to American masters such as Ansel Adams and beyond. Its Native American collection focuses on two disparate areas: the Southwest and the Eastern Woodlands. You'll find all the impressionist masters: Cézanne, Manet, Matisse, Monet, Picasso, Seurat and more. When this museum opens an exhibit, you know the exhibit is world-class. If you love art, this is your place.

★ NATIONAL MUSEUM OF FUNERAL HISTORY
415 Barren Springs Drive, Houston 77090
281-876-3063, www.nmfh.org

Why go? Spotlights the history of the funeral industry with unusual caskets, historic coaches and hearses. Exhibits include Day of the Dead memorabilia and a celebration of the lives and deaths of popes.

t Museums of Discovery

SAN JACINTO MONUMENT & MUSEUM
Photo: Allan C. Kimball

LaPORTE
★ San Jacinto Museum and Battleship Texas

San Jacinto: One Monument Circle, LaPorte 77571
281-479-2421, www.sanjacinto-museum.org

USS Texas: 3523 Texas 134, LaPorte 77571
281-479-2431
www.usstexasbb35.com and www.tpwd.state.tx.us/spdest/findadest/parks/battleship_texas/

Why go? Although these are two very different museums, they are situated adjacent to each other just east of Houston, and visiting one without seeing the other would be a travesty. The San Jacinto Museum celebrates the Battle of San Jacinto, fought on this ground back in 1836 when Texas won its independence from Mexico. The first thing you notice, and you notice it for miles and miles, is the monument with the big star on the top. The obelisk was purposely built to resemble the Washington Monument—but taller. The panoramic view from the top of the 570-foot monument shouldn't be missed. Among the things you will see is a bird's eye view of the Battleship Texas. Once

BATTLESHIP TEXAS: Photo: Texas Parks and Wildlife Department

the most powerful ship on the seas, the USS Texas was th... U.S. battleship to mount anti-aircraft guns, use radar and... a plane from its deck. Exhibits on the ship's second deck s... history of the ship, from its launch in 1912 to its decomm... in 1948, when it was presented to the state of Texas a... battleship memorial museum in the nation. Strolling it... peering up at the massive guns that launched shells as... Volkswagen is nothing short of impressive.

PORT ARTHUR
★ Museum of the Gulf Coast

700 Procter, Port Arthur 77640
409-982-7000, www.museumofthegulfcoast.org

Why go? Showcasing the history, natural hist... the coastal region between Houston and New (... Jurassic era to native daughter Janis Joplin.

ROCKPORT
★ Texas Maritime Museum

1202 Navigation Circle, Rockport 78382
361-729-1271, 866-729-2469, www.texasm...

Why go? This museum situated right... preserves the maritime history of Texas, f... commercial fishing and the oil and gas ind... who came to Texas across the sea land... with documents, maps, photographs, la... ships and artifacts such as ancient an... story of the offshore oil business is to... with interactive exhibits and a scale m... offshore drilling platform in history... collection of historically importan'... of them on display. From atop the...

TEXAS M...
visitors...
Port Ar...
museum...

★ Texas...
409 Sixth...
409-229-1...
MuseumA...

Why go...
U.S. Air Fo...
and devasta...
dinosaur dig...
Model Railr...

Texas...

North Texas

ADDISON

★ CAVANAUGH FLIGHT MUSEUM

4572 Claire Chennault Street, Addison 75001
972-380-8800, www.cavanaughflightmuseum.com

Why go? Displays historically significant vintage aircraft along with aviation artifacts and art. If you're flush, you can book a ride over the Dallas area in one of several planes in the collection.

BONHAM

★ SAM RAYBURN LIBRARY AND MUSEUM

800 W. Sam Rayburn Drive, Bonham 75418
903-583-2455, www.cah.utexas.edu/museums/rayburn_resources.php
Rayburn's home is also a museum at 890 W. TX Highway 56, Bonham 75418, 903-583-5558, www.visitsamrayburnhouse.com

Why go? Displays personal memorabilia of Sam Rayburn, who served as Speaker of the U.S. House of Representatives longer than any other person.

BUFFALO GAP

★ BUFFALO GAP HISTORIC VILLAGE

133 N. William Street, Buffalo Gap 79508
325-572-3365, www.buffalogap.com

Why go? Preserves the pioneer heritage of West Texas, from the 1870s to 1925, in a living-history museum with many original historic buildings and artifacts.

CLEBURNE

★ CHISHOLM TRAIL OUTDOOR MUSEUM

2929 W. Henderson, Cleburne 76033

817-648-1486, www.jcchisholmtrail.com

Why go? Outdoor museum with historic buildings, teepees, jail, log courthouse, blacksmith shop, stagecoach and other artifacts.

DALLAS

★ AFRICAN AMERICAN MUSEUM

Fair Park, 3536 Grand Avenue, Dallas 75210
214-565-9026, www.aamdallas.org

Why go? This is an impressive museum in an impressive building, built from ivory-colored stone in the shape of a cross. It's devoted to the preservation of African-American art, cultural and historical materials, with four vaulted galleries and a theater. There's a collection of African masks, sculpture and textiles; a fine-art collection showcases works by notable African-American artists from the 1800s to the present, while another gallery showcases folk art. Temporary exhibits feature art from around the country. The Texas Black Sports Hall of Fame is also housed in the museum, honoring greats such as Tony Dorsett and Richard "Night Train" Lane from pro football, Olympic track star Rafer Johnson, and women's basketball champ Fran Harris.

★ FRONTIERS OF FLIGHT MUSEUM

6911 Lemmon Avenue, Dallas 75209
214-350-1651, www.flightmuseum.com

Why go? Explores the history of aviation at Dallas Love Field, with several historic aircraft, important artifacts and a special section on lighter-than-air ships.

★ DALLAS MUSEUM OF ART

1717 N. Harwood, Dallas 75201
214-922-1200, www.dallasmuseumofart.org

Why go? Visitors here will discover an expansive collection of art from around the world, ancient to modern. The scope of the museum is remarkable. Where to start? Sub-Saharan African art, including rarely seen items of sculpture from the Congo. Ancient American art—3,000 years' worth. Asian art from second-century Buddhist works to Indian art from the 15th through the 19th century. Art from across the Pacific islands. European art from the past three centuries, along with Mediterranean works from 3000 BC to the fall of the

19th CENTURY YUPIK ESKIMO MASK: THE BAD SPIRIT OF THE MOUNTAIN. *Photo: Dallas Museum of Art, gift of Elizabeth H. Penn*

Roman Empire. Contemporary art and modern photographic art from the likes of masters such as Diane Arbus. The museum goes out of its way to engage visitors with a broad array of activities, programs and special exhibitions during the year. Among them are the Thursday Night Live jazz sessions; the Arts and Letters Live series, featuring noted authors and actors; and the Center for Creative Connections, which features interactive experiences for people of all ages.

★ MUSEUM OF NATURE AND SCIENCE
Nature Building: 3535 Grand Avenue, Dallas 75210
Science Building: 1318 S. Second Avenue, Dallas 75210
Planetarium: 1620 First Avenue, Dallas 75210
All in Fair Park, 214-428-5555, www.natureandscience.org

Why go? Here's a museum so big it needs three buildings to house it all. They're all at a convenient location in Fair Park. Formed in 2006 with the merger of the Dallas Museum of Natural History, the Science Place and the Dallas Children's Museum, the museum has one area specifically for children, with hands-on exhibits that allow kids to practice being a firefighter or to dress up in costumes and create their own characters. City children may be surprised to learn that milk and eggs come from farms; here they can check out a replica chicken coop or milk a replica cow. Other areas allow visitors to learn about their own bodies or how dinosaur bones are discovered; to view the bones of a giant mammoth that lived 20,000 years ago; or to spy on live ants, lizards, turtles and snakes. The museum even hosts Sleepover Nights. And take a step outside, where you can wander along the Lagoon Nature Walk to see exotic plants and dozens of species of birds.

★ NASHER SCULPTURE GARDEN

2001 Flora Street, Dallas 75201
214-242-5100, www.nashersculpturecenter.org

Why go? One of Texas' newest art museums, the Nasher opened its doors in 2003 to feature the collection of Ray and Patsy Nasher. The museum has an amazing collection of 20th-century sculpture in a beautiful building and a lush landscaped garden. You'll find works by such masters as Rodin, modern artists such as Picasso and contemporary artists such as Lichtenstein. Two of the Nasher's signature works are "Tending, (Blue)," James Turrell's enclosed skyscape designed and built especially for the site, and Jonathan Borofsky's 100-foot-tall "Walking to the Sky." But wait, there's more: Calder, de Kooning, Degas, Gauguin, Giacometti, Johns, Koons, Lichtenstein, Matisse, Miró, Oldenburg, Warhol. The fact that none of these artists needs a first name tells you just how legendary they are and how truly impressive this collection is.

The building, designed by famed architect Renzo Piano, is open and filled with natural light, merging into the outdoor garden, enclosed by travertine walls and planted with a wide variety of trees to provide an oasis in the middle of the city. As you wander around, you discover the foliage serves another purpose, creating virtual rooms to fulfill Nasher's vision of a "roofless" museum. The Nasher also features traveling exhibits and children's days full of various art activities on Saturdays.

★ Sixth Floor Museum at Dealey Plaza
411 Elm Street, Dallas 75202
214-747-6660, www.jfk.org

Why go? This unique museum is on the sixth and seventh floors of the former Texas School Book Depository building (now the Dallas County Administration Building) overlooking Dealey Plaza in Dallas. Lee Harvey Oswald fired the shots that killed President

SNIPER'S PERCH. *Photo: Sixth Floor Museum*

John F. Kennedy from the sixth floor of this very building, and it is the second-most-visited historic site in Texas (after the Alamo). Drawing from more than 25,000 items in its collection, the museum displays hundreds of photographs, films and artifacts on the early 1960s, focusing on the events surrounding the assassination on Nov. 22, 1963, and its aftermath. Among the exhibits is the famed Abraham Zapruder film considered the definitive documentation of JFK's assassination. Another video shows an interview with Bob Jackson, the *Dallas Times Herald* photographer who filmed Jack Ruby shooting Oswald. Another exhibit is a scale model of Dealey Plaza created by the FBI and used by the Warren Commission in its investigation into the assassination. One of the preserved areas is certain to send chills up your spine: the sniper's perch from which the fatal shots were fired. Recent additions include a bookstore and café, and you can also purchase a cell phone walking tour that guides you through Dallas sites relevant to the assassination.

DENTON

★ HISTORICAL PARK OF DENTON COUNTY

317 W. Mulberry, Denton 76201
940-349-2865, http://dentoncounty.com/dept/main.asp?Dept=128

Why go? Includes the Courthouse-on-the-Square Museum; the Bayless-Selby House Museum, a restored Victorian beauty that offers lectures and exhibits about the Victorian area; and the Denton County African American Museum, focusing on the history of the historic Quakertown neighborhood, where black residents were displaced for a city park in 1921.

FORT WORTH

★ AMON CARTER MUSEUM

3501 Camp Bowie Boulevard, Fort Worth 76107
817-738-1933, www.cartermuseum.org

Why go? This museum is the legacy of Fort Worth's legendary businessman and philanthropist Amon Carter, one of Fort Worth's leading citizens. His will stipulated that it be founded to house his collection of Western paintings and sculpture by Frederic Remington and Charles M. Russell, as well as to showcase the best of American art in a museum that would be free to everyone. To anyone who loves the West, the Remingtons alone are breathtaking. "A Dash for the Timber" right here? Gives you goosebumps. It's one of the most comprehensive collections of Western art in the country, but the museum isn't limited to those two icons. They share space in Philip Johnson's elegant building with paintings by Winslow Homer, Thomas Eakins and Georgia O'Keefe, just to name a few. In fact, the permanent collection has more than 200,000 objects showcasing a broad spectrum of American art and photography that rotate on a regular basis. Photography has become a big deal here: The collection is vast, and building expansions have provided a conservation center and a climate-controlled vault for the photos. Recent exhibitions have focused on great American photographers such as Berenice Abbott, Ansel Adams, Walker Evans and Margaret Bourke-White. The Amon Carter's library also houses a fascinating collection of illustrated books.

★ KIMBELL ART MUSEUM

3333 Camp Bowie Boulevard, Fort Worth 76107
817-332-8451, www.kimbellart.org

Why go? Neighboring the Amon Carter is another special Fort Worth art destination in the city's Cultural District. The Kimbell, established in 1972 by Kay and Velma Kimbell, has a small collection of quality art from the third millennium B.C. to the mid-20th century in an innovative, acclaimed building. A visitor is treated to works ranging from Fra Angelico to Cézanne, from Egyptian and Roman antiquities to Mayan art, from Asian to African decorative

"STANDING DIGNITARY," PRE-COLUMBIAN PERUVIAN ART.
Photo: Kimbell Art Museum

arts. Rembrandt or Picasso, anyone? Matisse? Mondrian? Maori figurines? Impressed yet? How about walking over to look at "The Torment of Saint Anthony," Michelangelo's first painting? It's one of only four the Italian master is known to have painted, and it's right here in Texas and not in the Uffizi Gallery in Florence. The complete collection is a relatively small 350 works, but the deal at the Kimbell is quality over quantity. The architecture alone makes the Kimbell a destination, with its barrel-vaulted roofs that flood the interior with natural light. It was designed by legendary architect Louis Kahn, and architect Renzo Piano was selected to design the museum's first major expansion. The museum's second-floor café and courtyard is a popular choice for locals who lunch.

★ MODERN ART MUSEUM

3200 Darnell Street, Fort Worth 76107
817-738-9215, www.themodern.org

Why go? It's the architecture of the Modern—the third in the Fort Worth Cultural District's trio of iconic museums—that is the first thing you notice. You just can't ignore Tadao Ando's glass pavilions that appear to float serenely on a calm pond. Nor can you ignore the monumental seven-story-tall steel sculpture by Richard Serra that towers over the museum outside, a magnet for kids and adults alike who are delighted to discover the way the sculpture echoes any sound made inside it. The focus here is on modern and contemporary art, from Picasso to Warhol and way beyond. The permanent collection holds more than 2,600 works, displayed on a rotating basis, by the likes of Anselm Kiefer, Jackson Pollock, Gerhard Richter, Susan Rothenberg, Andres Serrano and many more. It doesn't matter what floats your pavilion, you'll find it here: Abstract expressionism, pop art, minimalism and other art movements are represented in paintings, photography, sculpture and video. Gallery space is on two floors, a portion dedicated to that permanent collection and a portion to major traveling exhibits. The Café at the Modern draws food-lovers as well as art-lovers for its innovative brunch and lunch menu as well as weekly dinners.

★ MUSEUM OF SCIENCE AND HISTORY
includes **Cattle Raisers Museum**
1600 Gendy Street, Fort Worth 76107
817-255-9300 or 888-255-9300, www.fortworthmuseum.org

Why go? Looking up at a dinosaur is always educational and entertaining—even more so when the bones have been found nearby, and this museum has several of those. But that's only the beginning here—you can even create your own dinosaur on a computer screen. You can learn about energy from interactive multimedia exhibits, play in several studios that mix creativity and science or visit a separate Children's Museum area that has hands-on exhibits indoors and out, including live reptiles. The Noble Planetarium is also part of the museum, with an interactive program that makes it different from the usual star theaters – along with a program from the Cattle Raisers Museum, a bonus multi-media experience newly added to the complex. And that dome-looking cap atop one of the museum wings? That's the Omni Theater, which uses state-of-the art projection and oversized film for a special experience. Even the gift shop is atypical, offering educational items that relate to the exhibits.

★ NATIONAL COWGIRL MUSEUM AND HALL OF FAME

1720 Gendy Street, Fort Worth 76107
817-336-4475 or 800-476-3263, www.cowgirl.net

Photo: National Cowgirl Hall of Fame

Why go? Once tucked away in a library basement in the little Panhandle town of Hereford, the museum found a grander home in Fort Worth in 2002, and its large, handsome building is worthy of those being honored inside. Visitors are greeted by the "High Desert Princess," a life-size sculpture by Mehl Lawson showing a cowgirl standing next to her quarter horse, her riding coat blowing in the wind. Look around. You'll notice a huge mural of five cowgirls galloping toward the viewer, as well as several bas relief sculptures on the upper façade. Inside, the large, columned rotunda reminds visitors of a Greek temple. This museum preserves the history of women in the West, whether artists, performers, rodeo competitors, ranchers or pioneers. The Hall of Fame honors nearly 200 of them, from Hollywood's Dale Evans to the Supreme Court's Sandra Day O'Connor, from sharpshooter Annie Oakley to pioneer rancher Hallie Stillwell. You'll see hundreds of period photographs, guitars, sculptures, old posters, clothing, belt buckles, pistols, even pink boots. Here's one exhibit you won't find at any other Texas museum: You can ride a bucking bronco—well, it's a life-size bucking model of one—and get a 10-second video of your ride for posterity.

★ SID RICHARDSON MUSEUM OF WESTERN ART

309 Main Street, Fort Worth 76102
817-332-6554 or 888-332-6554, www.sidrichardsonmuseum.org

Why go? Remarkably, the Amon Carter isn't the only museum in Fort Worth that has paintings by premier Western artists Frederick Remington and Charles M. Russell in its collection, created from the legacy left by the remarkably successful wildcatter-philanthropist Sid Richardson. The same is true here, in a replica 1895 building that is one of the top attractions on the historic downtown Sundance Square. The museum also offers a variety of educational programs for adults and children.

FREDERICK REMINGTON'S "THE PUNCHER."
Photo: Sid Richardson Museum

★ TEXAS CIVIL WAR MUSEUM

760 Jim Wright Freeway N.
Fort Worth 76108

GOWN EXHIBIT. *Photo: Texas Civil War Museum*

817-246-2323, www.texascivilwarmuseum.com

Why go? Housed in a plantation-style building and comprising three galleries totaling 15,000 square feet, the museum boasts of having the most comprehensive collection of Civil War artifacts west of the Mississippi. One gallery features Civil War military items; another showcases a Victorian dress collection. An exhibit from the United Daughters of the Confederacy's Texas collection includes more than 60 flags, most from Texas units that fought for the Confederacy. Some exhibits remind visitors that this was the bloodiest conflict ever fought by Americans: a Bible soaked in the blood of the soldier who carried it; several items with bullet holes, including a powder flask. Several artifacts on display belonged to Texan Walter Williams, the last surviving Civil War veteran, who died in 1959 at the age of 117. You can even see a sword owned by General U.S. Grant. Or you can sample a piece of hardtack, a staple of military units during the war. It's made by the same bakery that supplied the Union army at the time.

★ TEXAS COWBOY HALL OF FAME

128 E. Exchange Avenue, Fort Worth 76164
817-626-7131, www.texascowboyhalloffame.com

Why go? How about them cowboys? No, not the ones who play football down the road, but the ranch hands and rodeo riders who helped shape the history and legend of Texas. They're honored at this museum in Fort Worth's Stockyards National Historic District. The emphasis here is on rodeo stars, but you'll also find other Texas legends, including baseball's Nolan Ryan, musician

Willie Nelson and popular physician Dr. James "Red" Duke, who may wear the most famous cowboy hat in all the state. But don't think this is just some hall with a passel of plaques on the walls. Look around and you'll see all sorts of horse-drawn wagons used in ranching; footwear and photographs telling the story of Justin Boots; Chisholm Trail artifacts such as branding irons, maps and cowboy clothing. And kids wondering what life was like on an Old West cattle drive can pack and saddle a horse, learn about brands, stock a chuck wagon, or dig in sawdust for arrowheads.

IRVING

★ NATIONAL SCOUTING MUSEUM

1329 W. Walnut Hill Lane, Irving 75038
972-580-2100 or 800-303-3047, www.bsamuseum.org

Why go? This is the official museum of the Boy Scouts of America. Over scouting's 100-plus years, according to the museum, some 110 million youngsters have taken that oath to honor God and their country, to help others and to keep themselves strong in all ways. Artist Norman Rockwell may have done more to promote scouting than any other single individual, and some of his paintings—along with a diorama explaining his creative process—are among the art works presented here. A film shows the history of scouting; another exhibit focuses on the annual Jamborees; another allows visitors to participate in interactive displays that show what scouts do to earn awards. Race on a pinewood derby track, learn to identify animal tracks, go spelunking in a cave, experience the thrill of virtual skydiving.

THURBER

★ W.K. GORDON CENTER FOR INDUSTRIAL HISTORY OF TEXAS

65258 Interstate 20 (Exit 367), Mingus 76463
254-968-1886, www.tarleton.edu/gordoncenter

Why go? Now a ghost town, Thurber was once the largest city between Fort Worth and El Paso. Made up of immigrant workers from several countries, it was a company town, owned entirely by the Texas & Pacific Coal Co. A leader in the labor union movement, it also became the only completely unionized town in the world. The Gordon Center—often referred to as the Ghost Town Museum—examines the impact of the brick, coal and petroleum industries on the area, with artifacts, films, photos and reconstructions of the town's structures.

VERNON
★ RED RIVER VALLEY MUSEUM
4600 College Drive, Vernon 76384
940-553-1848, www.redrivervalleymuseum.org

Why go? Something for everyone: historical exhibits, a big-game collection, Indian artifacts, fossils, sculpture, gem and rock collections, fine arts—including a collection of works by sculptor Electra Waggoner Biggs, who once co-owned the Waggoner Ranch—the Great Western Trail and living-history programs.

DAY OF THE DEAD EXHIBIT.
Photo: Museum of the Americas

WEATHERFORD
★ MUSEUM OF THE AMERICAS
216 Fort Worth Highway (US Highway 180), Weatherford 76086
817-341-8668,
www.museumoftheamericas.com

Why go? This modest space is crammed with artifacts, crafts and folk art of native peoples of the Western Hemisphere, from the Inuit and Northwest Coast natives to the Yamana of Tierra del Fuego.

★ NATIONAL VIETNAM WAR MUSEUM

12685 Mineral Wells Highway (US 180), Weatherford 76088
940-664-3918 or 940-325-4003
www.nationalvnwarmuseum.org

Why go? Promotes an understanding of the controversial conflict and honors those who served. Most exhibits are outside, including a replica of the Vietnam War Memorial Wall. Interactive exhibits are featured in the new visitor center.

WICHITA FALLS

★ Museum of North Texas History

720 Indiana Avenue, Wichita Falls 76301
940-322-7628, www.month-ntx.org

Why go? Educational exhibits showcase the area's past with artifacts, books, maps and photographs, along with a World War I exhibit at Kickapoo Airport and a functioning Curtiss Jenny aircraft. Includes county archives.

Texas Panhandle Plains

AMARILLO

★ AMARILLO MUSEUM OF ART

2200 S. Van Buren Street, Amarillo 79109
806-371-5050, www.amarillomuseumofart.org

Why go? Collections and temporary exhibitions in a variety of media and periods, with emphasis on American works on paper and photographs post-1945. The museum boasts an extensive gallery of Asian art. And admission is free every third Thursday of the month.

★ AMERICAN QUARTER HORSE HALL OF FAME AND MUSEUM

2601 Interstate 40 E., Amarillo 79104

GRAND HALL. *Photo: American Quarter Horse Museum*

806-376-5181, www.aqha.com

Why go? If you love horses, this museum is for you. Even if you're not that enamored of speedy equines and the folks who raise and ride them, check out this place just for the building—it's awesome, inside and out. The Grand Hall is a majestic space with wooden beams, massive stone columns towering way above you and plaques honoring the Hall of Fame members (both horses and people). Galleries offer bronzes and paintings, information about quarter-horse bloodlines, a diorama on what makes a quarter horse unique, a stable with information on how to care for the horses and an animated large-animal veterinarian and talking horse (Doc and Two Bits, respectively) that give you tips on quarter-horse health issues. You'll even find one interactive exhibit where you can compare your own lung capacity with that of a quarter horse. Theaters offer films on Hall of Fame inductees and world champions.

★ DON HARRINGTON DISCOVERY CENTER

1200 Streit Drive, Amarillo 79106
806-355-9547, www.dhdc.org

Why go? The folks behind the Harrington Center love to teach children, and it shows. Everywhere you go are interactive exhibits that engage and educate; even toddlers will find something to keep them amused and challenged. The scope is quite broad, from birds of prey to the planets and space, from mathematics to physics. Want an unusual birthday party for your kids? Hold it here and get all these educational exhibits and a Space Theater show included, along with cupcakes and the child's name projected on the Space Theater dome. The museum will even baby-sit for you: Its Night at the Museum provides dinner and special programs for children in the evening.

★ KWAHADI MUSEUM OF THE AMERICAN INDIAN

9151 Interstate 40 E., Amarillo 79120
806-335-3175, www.kwahadi.com

Why go? Showcases the cultures of the Plains and Pueblo Indians with fine art, craftwork and artifacts, along with performances of native dances. Features the work of artist Thomas E. Mails and sculptor Tom Knapp. The gift shop features hundreds of handcrafted items by Native American artists and artisans.

★ TEXAS PHARMACY MUSEUM

1300 Coulter Street, Amarillo 79106
806-356-4000
www.ttuhsc.edu/sop/prospective/visitors/museum.aspx

Why go? In the basement of the Texas Tech School of Pharmacy you'll find artifacts, products, literature and art illuminating the history of pharmacy.

CANADIAN

★ RIVER VALLEY PIONEER MUSEUM

118 N. Second Street, Canadian 79014
806-323-6548, www.rivervalleymuseum.org

Why go? Traces the history of settlement in the Canadian River Valley of the High Plains with artifacts, art, mobile displays, murals and photos, including the glass-negative collection of Julius Born, who was the town photographer in the early part of the 20th century. Hosts many traveling exhibits.

BUNKHOUSE EXHIBIT.
Photo: River Valley Pioneer Museum

OIL PATCH EXHIBIT, PANHANDLE PLAINS HISTORICAL MUSEUM. *Photo: Allan C. Kimball*

CANYON

★ PANHANDLE PLAINS HISTORICAL MUSEUM

2503 Fourth Avenue, Canyon 79015
806-651-2244, www.panhandleplains.org

Why go? It's not the largest museum in Texas, or the most spectacular, but it's close. This museum houses information on nearly everything essential to what makes Texas special. Consider that it has a skeleton of a predator dinosaur, mouth open and poised to clamp down on your little head. That you can wander through 14,000 years of history, seeing how people lived and dressed over the centuries. That it has a fascinating gallery dedicated to geology. How about an old oil wellhead, complete with engines, and a Depression-era truck? Even more artifacts from the oil patch are on display on the second floor, along with a 1930s filling station and several art galleries. It also has the most comprehensive art collection in northwest Texas. Not enough to impress? How about the fact that it has an entire pioneer town down one hallway? How about Billy Dixon's Sharps rifle? (He's the guy who ended the Second Battle of Adobe Walls by making a legendary 1,200-yard shot that marksmen still talk about.) That rifle is among more than a thousand items spanning five centuries in the firearms gallery alone. And look: There's legendary Comanche chief Quanah Parker's headdress. This is all the real thing.

DALHART

★ XIT Museum
108 E. Fifth Street, Dalhart 79022
806-244-5390, www.xitmuseum.com

Why go? Exhibits on the famed XIT Ranch (once three million acres large), pioneer railroading, firearms, county sheriffs, local history, and area wildlife. You'll even discover a historic airplane in one room.

DUMAS

★ Window on the Plains Museum and Art Center
Museum: 1820 S. Dumas Avenue, 806-935-3113
Art Center: 1810 S. Dumas Avenue, 806-935-5312
Dumas 79029, www.dumasmuseumandartcenter.org

Why go? These two neighboring museums provide an excellent look at area history and give local artists a place to show their works. The museum houses hundreds of historical artifacts—but they aren't displayed in typical exhibit cases, they're in their natural setting along a turn-of-the-century street. A stroll down the street is like taking a trip in a time machine: a general store and post office, a doctor's office, a ranch house, a blacksmith shop, a home and a camp-meeting tent—all fully stocked with period furniture, appliances, tools and toys. The dining room in the home is set for a family of four, with a china collection in a nearby cabinet and a crank telephone on the wall, and the ranch house kitchen has a pot ready to boil on its grand black-and-pewter wood stove.

LUBBOCK
★ NATIONAL RANCHING HERITAGE CENTER
3121 Fourth Street, Lubbock 79409
806-742-0498, www.depts.ttu.edu/ranchhc/

Why go? When outsiders think of Texas, they usually think of two things: oil and ranching. Oil is featured at several museums, but here's one of the few dedicated to ranching. On the 30-acre grounds are gathered 38 original ranch structures from around the state. One exhibit that is certain to fascinate is a collection of Western-themed toys; those who remember Hopalong Cassidy, Roy Rogers and Davy Crockett with nostalgia will be in heaven here. You can even build a fort with giant Lincoln Logs. Other exhibits focus on historic firearms, branding irons, custom boots and spurs; there's even a rare pair of woolly chaps. One gallery features an entire saddlemaker's shop; another displays a century of saddles. One new exhibit shoecases a Model T Ford. More artifacts, paintings and sculpture await in other galleries.

McLEAN
★ DEVIL'S ROPE MUSEUM
100 Kingsley Street, McLean 79057
806-779-2225, www.barbwiremuseum.com

Why go? This small museum is important for its focus on barbed wire—dubbed the "Devil's Rope" by the open-range cattlemen who hated the new product that would ultimately tame the West. Only the railroad had a bigger impact on ranching in Texas. Here you can see thousands of different types of barbed wire, hundreds of

BARBED WIRE HAT. *Photo: Devil's Rope Museum*

tools made to handle it, an 1893 fence-repair wagon and an exhibit on barbed wire used in warfare. Watch a machine make barbed wire and be amazed at the barbed-wire cowboy hat—ouch! Other exhibits focus on ranching history, the evolution of the cowboy, cattle brands, trail-drive maps and more. Speaking of more, the museum is on historic Route 66, so it also has a space dedicated to art and artifacts relating to the "Mother Road"—road signs, advertising items, a typical Route 66 greasy-spoon café and a cute little restored Phillips 66 gas station, reported to have been the company's first in Texas.

POST

★ GARZA COUNTY HISTORICAL MUSEUM

119 N. Avenue N., Post 79356
806-495-2207, www.ccaheritagehouse.com/museum.html

Why go? Exhibits on C.W. Post, the cereal magnate who founded the city as a utopian community, as well as on various Native American tribes, area pioneers, dinosaur fossils and the like. The museum is housed in the historic Post Sanitarium.

South Texas

ALAMO HEIGHTS

★ Barney Smith's Toilet Seat Art Museum

239 Abiso Avenue, Alamo Heights 78209
210-824-7791
www.unusualmuseums.org/toilet

Why go? Plumber Barney Smith has collaged, painted and embellished more than a thousand toilet seat lids. Among the unsual seats are parts of a toilet from Saddam Hussein's palace, $1 million in shredded cash, and a piece of the *Challenger* shuttle.

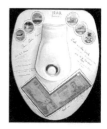

SADDAM HUSSEIN TOILET.
Photo: Allan C. Kimball

BRACKETTVILLE

★ Fort Clark Guardhouse Museum

McClearend Road, Fort Clark Springs, Brackettville 78832
830-563-2493
www.fortclark.com

Why go? Within a 1600-acre resort and real-estate development off US Highway 90 is a museum preserving the military history of this historic fort and the pioneer history of the area, with a special focus on Buffalo Soldiers and Seminole-

SEMINOLE SCOUT EXHIBIT.
Photo: Allan C. Kimball

Negro Indian scouts.

BROWNSVILLE
★ Brownsville Museum of Fine Art
660 E. Ringgold Street, Brownsville 78520
956-542-0941
www.brownsvillemfa.org

Why go? Regional art from South Texas and Mexico; traveling shows from partner museums; classes, concerts and lectures.

★ Rio Grande Wing, Commemorative Air Force Museum
955 S. Minnesota Avenue, Brownsville 78521
956-541-8585, www.rgvwingcaf.com

Why go? Aircraft, artifacts, photographs from World War II.

DEL RIO
★ Whitehead Memorial Museum
1308 S. Main Street, Del Rio 78840
830-774-7568, www.whiteheadmuseum.com

JUDGE ROY BEAN GRAVE. *Photo: Allan C. Kimball*

Why go? The Whitehead is an ambitious museum for a city as small as Del Rio. It includes more than 20 exhibit sites, some in historic buildings and some outdoors, over two acres. The focus is on area history, from the office of the first Hispanic physician in the city to folk art. Running through the grounds is the San Felipe Irrigation Ditch, the acequia built in 1871 to water crops. Here is the Perry Store, a historical landmark and once the largest mercantile between San Antonio and El Paso. Over there is a log cabin displaying items used by early pioneers; nearby, a collection of barbed wire and Indian artifacts next to a fully stocked livery stable and a railroad station. Skipping forward a few years, you'll find a display on the border radio station run by Hal Patton: With a broadcast tower in Mexico, XERA was the world's most powerful station, enabling legendary disc jockey Wolfman Jack's howl to be heard as far away as Canada. There's also a replica of the famed Jersey Lilly Saloon— and, speaking of the Jersey Lilly, the museum is the burial site of Judge Roy Bean, perhaps the main reason to visit.

EDINBURG
★ MUSEUM OF SOUTH TEXAS HISTORY

200 N. Closner Boulevard, Edinburg 78541
956-383-6911, www.mosthistory.org

Why go? Few places in the United States offer the kind of blended culture the Rio Grande Valley does, and this museum provides a look at that heritage. The Rio Grande is the primary focus here, as indicated by three of the main exhibits—River Frontier, River Highway and River Crossroads. Artifacts and multimedia presentations abound. Take a gander at prehistoric fossils, steamboat artifacts, Spanish treasures and battlefield items. Listen to conjunto music. Walk on the bow of a steamship. Visit a railroad station. Watch historic films. Outside you can visit a 1910-era jail with rotating exhibits on the ground floor and a second-floor exhibit honoring Freddy Gonzales, a local Medal of Honor winner for his service in Vietnam. Beyond the jail are a park area with sculpture; a windmill, tank and water pump; and a walking trail with native animal tracks and native plants.

KINGSVILLE
★ JOHN E. CONNER MUSEUM

905 W. Santa Gertrudis Avenue, Kingsville 78363

361-593-2810

Why go? Historical displays, from fossils to the multicultural heritage of the region.

★ King Ranch Museum

405 N. Sixth Street, Kingsville 78363

361-595-1881, www.king-ranch.com/museum.html

Why go? Repository of artifacts from one of the most important ranches in Texas.

LANGTRY

★ Judge Roy Bean Visitor's Center

U.S. 90 West/Texas Loop 25, Langtry 78871

432-291-3340, www.txdot.gov/travel/information_centers.htm

Why go? You've read about Judge Roy Bean, the self-proclaimed Law West of the Pecos, who dispensed that law from his saloon in Langtry; now you can tread upon the same boards the old judge trod. This is it—the real Jersey Lilly Saloon. And just up one small

JERSEY LILLY SALOON. *Photo: Allan C. Kimball*

hill is Bean's home, labeled the Opera House now. Up another small hill is a historic windmill surrounded by an impressive cactus garden. The flora in the garden are labeled; you'll find just about any plant you are likely to see in your travels in South and West Texas. Inside the visitor center is a museum dedicated to Judge Bean; his life and the history of the small village are told in six narrated dioramas. Also on display are some of Bean's personal items, such as his law book and his pistol. The visitor center is a Texas Highway Department Travel Information Center, where you can also get brochures on attractions from around the state.

LAREDO
★ MUSEUMS OF VILLA ANTIGUA

Villa Antigua Border Heritage Museum: 810 Zaragoza Street, Laredo 78040

956-727-0977, www.webbheritage.org

Republic of the Rio Grande Museum: 1005 Zaragoza Street, Laredo 78040

956-727-3480, www.webbheritage.org

Why go? The Border Heritage Museum showcases the Mexico-U.S. border legacy with some artifacts and lots of art. Most of the exhibits here change every several months. The Republic of the Rio Grande Museum is housed in one of the oldest buildings in Laredo, at historic San Agustín Plaza. This museum tells the story of the ill-fated Republic of the Rio Grande in 1840, when the area between the Rio Grande and the Nueces River was in dispute. The Republic gives Laredo the distinction of having had seven flags fly over it instead of the usual six for the rest of Texas.

McALLEN
★ INTERNATIONAL MUSEUM OF ART AND SCIENCE

1900 Nolana Avenue, McAllen 78504

956-682-1564, www.imasonline.org

Why go? Educational displays of art and natural science with a hands-on children's area and a theater.

PORT ISABEL
★ Museums of Port Isabel

317 E. Railroad Avenue, Port Isabel 78578
956-943-7602, www.portisabelmuseums.com

Why go? A complex of three museums tells the story of this scenic end of Texas. The Treasures of the Gulf Museum focuses on the Spanish fleet of 1554 that wrecked along the Texas coast near here, with many of the artifacts and treasures from the ships on display. The Port Isabel Historic Museum, in an 1899 building that originally housed a dry-goods store and home, focuses on the later settlers, from the early Spanish to the Anglos, through the Mexican War to more modern times. Among the exhibits are one of the largest collections of artifacts from the Mexican War, including cannon balls, swords and uniforms. You can also visit the 1852 Port Isabel Lighthouse, the only one in Texas open to the public, along with the Keepers Cottage.

THE ALAMO. Photo: Allan C. Kimball

SAN ANTONIO
★ The Alamo

300 Alamo Plaza, San Antonio 78205
210-225-1391
www.thealamo.org

Why go? Everyone remembers the Alamo, including people in faraway lands.

This shrine—Texas' most-visited historic site—is a must-stop on any Texas trip. The mission, established in 1724, is where a small band of rebel Texicans held off massive Mexican army for 13 days until falling on March 6, 1836. Every defender was killed. This famed battlefield with its familiar mission façade is in the middle of downtown

a

DAVID CROCKETT'S EMBROIDERED VEST. *Photo: The Alamo*

San Antonio, with a huge mall next door that has an IMAX theater regularly showing an Alamo film. First time visitors are surprised at how small the Alamo is because much of the original mission is gone, and most of the grounds are given over to landscaping and history talks, a gift shop, and the Daughters of the Republic of Texas Library. Inside the hallowed walls, several exhibits tell the story of the Alamo and of Texas independence. Among the artifacts you can see are David Crockett's rifle and fanciful embroidered vest. Even the walls themselves display history, with their silently eloquent bullet holes.

★ INSTITUTE OF TEXAN CULTURES

801 E. Durango Boulevard, San Antonio 78205
210-458-2300, www.texancultures.utsa.edu/

Why go? This immense museum showcases artifacts, dioramas

PIONEER FABRIC EXHIBIT. *Photo: Allan C. Kimball*

and photographs from the more than 20 cultures that settled Texas and made it what it is today, one of the most diverse states in the nation. The 26-screen Dome Show Theater presents multimedia stories of Texans. A more up-close-and-personal look at Texan cultures happens in the Back 40, an outdoor learning area with an adobe house, a barn, a fort, a log cabin and a one-room schoolhouse, all from the 19th century. Interpreters here give visitors a glimpse into frontier life. Areas inside also feature volunteers, who demonstrate pioneer skills such as spinning wool. In the main hall are exhibits—many of them interactive—on such widely varied subjects as Wendish wedding customs, writing in Chinese, Japanese Americans in World War II detainment camps, how to dance a Czech polka, the black Seminoles and the Danish Texan responsible for Mount Rushmore. The museum also hosts a huge Texas Folklife Festival in June of each year, showcasing the distinctive art, clothing, dances, food, music and wares of the various cultures of Texas.

★ McNay Art Museum

6000 N. New Braunfels, San Antonio 78209
210-824-5368, www.mcnayart.org

Why go? One of the Southwest's most distinguished art collections, from medieval to modern, built on the collection of Marion McNay and housed in the mansion that served as her home. Includes an impressive theater-arts collection.

★ SAN ANTONIO MUSEUM OF ART

200 W. Jones Avenue, San Antonio 78215
210-978-8100, www.samuseum.org

Why go? Large collection of works from a broad range of cultures and history, including one of the most comprehensive collections of Latin American art in the United States and a broad Asian collection, particularly strong in Chinese ceramics and other decorative arts. It's all housed in the former Lone Star Brewery, overlooking the serene new Museum Reach section of the Riverwalk and accessible by river taxi.

★ TEXAS HIGHWAY PATROL MUSEUM

812 South Alamo Street
San Antonio 78205
210-231-6030
http://thpa.org/museum.
htm

Why go? Displays depicting state troopers through history.

Photo: Highway Patrol Museum

★ TEXAS RANGER MUSEUM AND BUCKHORN MUSEUM AND SALOON

318 E. Houston Street, San Antonio 78205
210-247-4000, www.buckhornmuseum.com

Why go? Located a couple blocks from the Alamo, the Ranger museum displays hundreds of Texas Ranger artifacts, including badges, firearms and photographs in a re-creation of a Western town, along with a Bonnie and Clyde exhibit. The Buckhorn features a collection of horns, antlers and stuffed wildlife from around the world in a historic saloon.

★ WITTE MUSEUM

3801 Broadway, San Antonio 78209
210-357-1900, www.wittemuseum.org

Why go? You shouldn't miss the Witte, San Antonio's top museum of culture, history and natural science. The Science Treehouse alone—four stories of exploratory delight for children—makes this a destination for families. Where else can a kid ride a bicycle along a raised cable, and do it safely? This place is overflowing with interactive exhibits teaching about the human body, energy, physics and more. Computers allow kids to become a character from *Star Trek* or to try their hand at kayaking or snowboarding. In other areas you'll find dinosaur skeletons, prehistoric Texas rock art, mummies, exhibits on wildlife and historic homes.

SARITA

★ KENEDY RANCH MUSEUM OF SOUTH TEXAS

200 E. La Parra Avenue, Sarita 78385
361-294-5751, www.kenedymuseum.org

Why go? Displays the history of the Kenedy family, the 400,000-acre Kenedy Ranch in the midst of the Wild Horse Desert and the cowboys and vaqueros who worked on the ranch.

UVALDE

★ JOHN NANCE GARNER MUSEUM

333 N. Park Street, Uvalde 78801
830-278-5018, www.cah.utexas.edu/museums/garner.php
Call or check website before visiting. The museum has been undergoing an extended renovation with an indeterminate reopening time; its interim home is at First State Bank, 200 E. Nopal.

Why go? Documents the history of "Cactus Jack" Garner, one of most powerful vice presidents in U.S. history during the Great Depression.

West Texas

ABILENE

★ FRONTIER TEXAS

625 N. First Street, Abilene 79601
325-437-2800, www.frontiertexas.com

Why go? Visitors relive the Old West of buffalo stampedes, Indian attacks and saloon shootouts in a big-screen multimedia theater with special effects.

★ THE GRACE MUSEUM

102 Cypress Street, Abilene 79601
325-673-4587, www.thegracemuseum.org

Why go? The historic Grace Hotel hosts three museums in one: an art museum, with five galleries housing mostly contemporary exhibits; a children's discovery area; and a third-floor history museum re-creating the Abilene of the past.

ALBANY

★ OLD JAIL ART CENTER

201 S. Second Street, Albany 76430
325-762-2269, www.theoldjailartcenter.org

Why go? Paintings by Klee, Modigliani, Picasso and Renoir locked up in a jail? You don't expect this, especially not in a tiny village of 1,921 on the eastern edge of West Texas—a hop, skip and a cow patty toss from Abilene. This two-story plain gray-limestone edifice was built in 1877 as the Shackelford County Jail, but today it houses an impressive, eclectic collection of modern masters like those mentioned above, along with British artists, works from the Taos School and the Fort Worth Circle, a small but impressive Asian collection, pre-Columbian pieces and contemporary sculpture scattered about the grounds. Don't let the bland exterior fool you; inside you will discover a modern, open space of 15,000 square feet that is the exact opposite of a jail and showcases the art perfectly. (The upstairs galleries, where temporary exhibits often feature the works of Texas artists, are housed in the former jail cells, left more in their original state.) A recent addition is historical—the Sallie Reynolds Matthews Historical Room and Watt Matthews Ranching Collection, a re-creation of rooms at the famed Lambshead Ranch, filled with family and ranching artifacts. If research is your thing, you'll find a full art library and archives from Albany, Shackelford County, Fort Griffin and Camp Cooper.

ALPINE

★ Museum of the Big Bend

On the Sul Ross University campus at Entrance Four on Hancock Drive, Alpine 79832

432-837-8143, www.sulross.edu/museum/

Why go? Everyone going to the Big Bend of Texas should stop by here to orient themselves to the history and culture of this vast region. The museum has been housed

in several locations at Sul Ross University over the years but now has the gorgeous red-rock McCoy Building to call home. Visitors take a walk through the history of the Big Bend, with artifacts and exhibits on Native Americans, Spanish explorers and Anglo

TRAILDRIVE EXHIBIT. Photo: Allan C. Kimball

pioneers and soldiers. Look up when you first walk in—there's a pterosaur flying over your head below the rafters. Spend some time looking at a wooden cart—it's a scale model of an oxcart, and you can barely imagine how it could have transported goods over vast distances. You'll also see historic maps, an entire room devoted to religious art, lots of arrowheads and other historic artifacts. The museum has extensive programs for children, including weekly classes, summer art camps and a Night at the Museum complete with flashlight tours and a planetarium visit.

EL PASO

★ CENTENNIAL MUSEUM AND CHIHUAHUAN DESERT GARDENS

On the University of Texas at El Paso campus
500 W. University Avenue, El Paso 79968
915-747-5565, www.museum.utep.edu

Why go? This was El Paso's first museum. Part of the University of Texas at El Paso, it's focused on the land and culture of the border. That's land as in rocks, not just geography, because UTEP began life as the Texas School of Mines and Metallurgy. As you might expect, the museum's Geology Gallery offers a comprehensive look at that mining history and at the volcanoes and earthquakes that formed the land, with exhibits of rocks and minerals of all sorts. Fossils and dinosaurs may be found over in the Paleontology Gallery. Yet another gallery looks at the region's various wildlife, from hummingbirds to roadrunners, scorpions to rattlesnakes. Dioramas, artifacts, documents and photographs showcase the cultural history, with exhibits focusing on the Native Americans who first populated the area. One display is of exquisite Mimbres pottery, rare in Texas museums. Out in the Desert Garden are more than two dozen interlocking garden areas holding more than 600 species of plants native to the Chihuahuan Desert, from goldenball leadtree to turpentine bush, including an extensive collection of cacti, some rare and endangered. "Rake Mark," an imposing abstract sculpture in red sandstone by Otto Rigan, invites extended contemplation, as does the Contemplative Garden.

★ El Paso Museum of Art

One Arts Festival Plaza, El Paso 79901
915-632-1707, www.elpasoartmuseum.org
   Why go? Collections of American, European and Mexican art, plus temporary exhibits, films and concerts.

★ El Paso Museum of History

510 N. Santa Fe Street, El Paso 79901
915-351-3588, www.ci.el-paso.tx.us/history
   Why go? El Paso means "The Pass," and the city wouldn't exist if it weren't for its position in the Franklin Mountains and

Chihuahuan Desert along the Rio Grande. Visitors will learn all about The Pass and how it has changed over the years. Exhibits focus on the original Native Americans who traveled through here, the international border and the history

AVIATION GALLERY. *Photo: El Paso Museum of History*

of the many cultures who settled here. Among the items visitors will see are a cannon from the Mexican Revolution, an oxcart, rifles, a wine vat made from cowhide, an exhibit on the Bobby Fuller Four music group, and a massive display on Spanish missions. The museum also hosts temporary historical exhibits.

★ Fort Bliss Museums

Fort Bliss Building 1735, Marshall Road, El Paso 79916
915-568-3390, www.bliss.army.mil/museum/fort_bliss_museum.htm

Why go? Several military museums on an active U.S. Army base, including a replica of historic Fort Bliss.

★ Insights El Paso Science Museum

505 N. Santa Fe Avenue, El Paso 79901
915-534-0000, www.insightselpaso.org

Why go? Makes science fun for kids with exhibits such as a Tesla coil and centrifugal force spinner.

★ National Border Patrol Museum

4315 Transmountain Road, El Paso 79924
915-759-6060, www.borderpatrolmuseum.com

Why go? The border between the U.S. and Mexico has never been such a hotly debated issue, and the U.S. Border Patrol is caught in the middle—literally. The job of the Border Patrol has never been more difficult or more dangerous, and its story is told at this small museum, from its beginnings in the Old West through Prohibition and World War II to today. Though relatively small, the museum is quite comprehensive. Visitors get to see not just vehicles, but helicopters and planes used by the Border Patrol over the years, various weapons and uniforms, as well as art. The historic photographs are compelling, and one exhibit honors the Border Patrol men and women who gave their lives during their service.

FORT DAVIS
★ Fort Davis National Historic Site

1 Lt. H.O. Flipper Drive (off Texas 118 and 17), Fort Davis 79734
432-426-3224, www.nps.gov/foda

FORT DAVIS OFFICERS' QUARTERS. *Photo: Allan C. Kimball*

Why go? This is the best-restored Indian Wars fort in the U.S. Park Service, and if all you know about such forts is what you've seen in the movies, this renowned facility will snap your head around. You won't find tall palisades, just a broad field tucked into a scenic canyon. It's not a desert; it's mild and green here most of the year. If you were a soldier and were going to be sent to Texas, this is where you wanted to come. On one side of the parade ground are the 1880s-era officers' quarters, inviting even 130 years after they were built. On the other side are enlisted barracks, and scattered around are the 1876 post hospital, sutler's store, armory, other historic buildings and a number of ruins. In the visitor center, a museum displays Army uniforms, weapons and equipment and tells the story of Lt. Henry Flipper, the first African American to graduate from West Point, who was stationed here. One of the barracks is restored with bunks and trunks and more uniforms; several of the officers' quarters are also fully furnished and restored. Peeking inside is like taking a step back in time.

LAJITAS
★ BARTON WARNOCK ENVIRONMENTAL EDUCATION CENTER
21800 Farm Road 170, Lajitas 79852
432-424-3327
www.tpwd.state.tx.us/spdest/findadest/parks/barton_warnock/

Why go? Inside and out, this is a fine museum stuck out in what seems like the middle of noplace, in the Chihuahuan Desert not far from the Rio Grande. This area was one of the most remote in America when it was first settled—it still is—and its population remains small. Named for a famed botanist from Big Bend, the center is part of the Big Bend Ranch State Park complex and tells the region's cultural and natural history. One of the most impressive exhibits is of a huge pterosaur skeleton—a flying reptile fearsome enough to contemplate but even more real when you realize that they soared from the very cliffs that loom behind the museum. The museum looks at 570 million years of geological history and the diverse landscapes—desert, river, and mountains—that make up the Big Bend. You'll find some artifacts, but mostly the story is told in displays, with historic documents and photographs. The desert garden offers a scenic walk among cactus, yucca and other native plants you will encounter in the Big Bend.

GEOLOGIC EXHIBIT AT BARTON WARNOCK ENVIRONMENTAL EDUCATION CENTER.
Photo: Earl Nottingham, Texas Parks and Wildlife Department

MARFA

★ Chinati Foundation
1 Cavalry Row, Marfa 79843
432-729-4362, www.chinati.org

Why go? Decide for yourself whether the massive outdoor concrete sculptures of founder Donald Judd look more like art or culverts, but this contemporary-art museum housed on the 340-acre site of former Fort D.A. Russell has put little Marfa on the cultural map. Focusing on large-scale installations that link the art with the vast surrounding landscape, the collection was originally devoted to the work of Judd, Dan Flavin and John Chamberlain but now includes works by several other noted contemporary artists, each in a separate building. Outdoor sculptures include the playful "Monument to the Last Horse" by Claes Oldenburg and Coosje van Bruggen. The museum features temporary exhibitions, too.

MIDLAND

★ Commemorative Air Force Airpower Museum
9600 Wright Drive, Midland 79706
432-567-3010, www.airpowermuseum.com

MAIN GALLERY. *Photo: Commemorative Air Force Museum*

Why go? Preserves the history of aviation in World War II with restored aircraft, art, artifacts and photographs, including 34 panels of WWII aircraft "nose art" cut from the planes' fuselages after the war. Also houses the American Combat Airman Hall of Fame.

★ MUSEUM OF THE SOUTHWEST

1705 W. Missouri Avenue, Midland 79701
432-683-2882, www.museumsw.org

Why go? This museum complex is actually three facilities: the Art Museum, the Children's Museum and the Blakemore Planetarium. The Art Museum, in the historic Turner House mansion, displays paintings and sculptures from ancient to modern, including many artists from the Taos School, detailed animal studies by John W. Audubon and rare Native American art and artifacts. Its sculpture garden is suitably impressive. The Art Museum also showcases an archaeological collection with items like arrowheads and prehistoric grinding stones. Exhibits in the Children's Museum are constantly changing and interactive, including a seven-station computer center with programs on a variety of careers. The centerpiece here is My

SCULPTURE GARDEN.
Photo: Museum of the Southwest

Town, a two-story city that enables children to explore and role-play in an animal hospital, a bank or a TV station.

★ PERMIAN BASIN PETROLEUM MUSEUM

1500 Interstate 20 W., Midland 79701

432-683-4403, www.petroleummuseum.org

Why go? Oil is big in this part of Texas. Real big. You can't drive anywhere without seeing derricks or pump jacks. Learn about it all here. Exhibits show the geological development of the Permian Basin—the world's thickest deposits of rocks, from the Permian geological period of about 230 million years ago—and how oil got to be in the ground. This museum doesn't mess around. Visitors get to see an oil boomtown and actual drilling rigs and derricks along with tools and equipment in a massive 40-acre outdoor exhibit. Inside, fly virtually with a pilot searching for pipeline leaks; feel the ground tremble with an explosive blast. The Petroleum Hall of Fame honors people who have made significant contributions to the industry. The museum is also home to the Chaparral Gallery, preserving the history of innovative race car driver and builder Jim Hall. Several of his aerodynamic cars are on display, including the Chaparral 2K that won the 1980 Indianapolis 500.

ODESSA

★ ODESSA METEOR CRATER MUSEUM

3100 Meteor Crater Road, Odessa 79764

432-381-0946, www.netwest.com/virtdomains/meteorcrater/About.htm

Why go? At the site of the second-largest crater in the United States, a visitor center has pieces of the meteor, other space artifacts and exhibits.

★ PRESIDENTIAL MUSEUM AND LEADERSHIP LIBRARY

4919 E. University Avenue, Odessa 79761

432-363-7737, www.thepresidentialmuseum.org

Why go? Dedicated to office of the presidency. Also on the grounds is the Odessa home where presidents George H.W. and George W. Bush lived in the late 1940s.

PECOS
★ WEST OF THE PECOS MUSEUM
First and Cedar Streets, Pecos 79772
432-445-5076, www.westofthepecosmuseum.com
Why go? Indoor and outdoor exhibits of West Texas history in an old hotel and saloon.

SAN ANGELO
★ MISS HATTIE'S BORDELLO MUSEUM
18 ½ E. Concho Avenue, San Angelo 76903
325-653-0570 (cafe), www.misshatties.com
Why go? The only things missing from this famed brothel near Fort Concho are Miss Hattie and her girls. Miss Hattie-themed cafe and saloon are nearby.

★ SAN ANGELO MUSEUM OF FINE ARTS
1 Love Street, San Angelo 76903
325-653-3333, www.samfa.org
Why go? Collection of visual arts and crafts in an innovative building on the banks of the Concho River. Focuses on American and Mexican art, along with American crafts featuring a strong ceramics collection.

Photo: Allan C. Kimball

TEXAS | POCKET GUIDE

Texas Landmark Saloons, Honky Tonks & Dance Halls

"The new pocket-size guide takes a Western swing throughout the state, hitting the best little places in Texas to kick up your heels and two-step." —*Fort Worth Star-Telegram.* 80 pages, paperback ISBN 1-892588-22-6. List $5.95

Texas Landmark Cafes

"You'll never go hungry if you pack this book, which covers the state's four major food groups: barbecue, steaks, Tex-Mex and pie." —*Dallas Morning News.* "Pocket-size gem." —*Houston Chronicle.* 88 pages, paperback. ISBN 1-892588-17-X. List $5.95

Texas Wineries

"One of the best on its subject." —*Sherman Herald-Democrat.* "Scattered throughout Texas, the wineries require a guide for visitors to find them. Fortunately, Barry Shlachter has done your legwork." —*Austin American-Statesman.* 96 pages, paperback. ISBN No. 1-892588-19-6. List $5.95.

Texas 107 Best Walks

"Each walk includes a brief description including length, degree of difficulty, location, best time to visit, what to look for, and how to obtain more information. Keep this one in the car." —*San Angelo Standard-Times.* 80 pages, paperback. ISBN 1-892588-24-1. List $5.95

Big Bend Guide

"Whether spending two days or 10, the guide provides the skinny on what to do, what to see and how to get there." —*Texas Highways Magazine.* "One of the best. Written with a touch of humor and an obvious love for Big Bend." —*Austin American Statesman.* 104 pages, paperback ISBN 1-892588-20-X. List $5.95